1874
BOSTON

1874

BOSTON

AND ITS NEIGHBORHOODS

By G.M. Towle

Illustrations By J. D. Woodward

Applewood Books

CARLISLE, MASSACHUSETTS

Cover Image: J. D. Woodward, Detail of *City of Boston* (From South Boston), 1874, Steel Engraving

Thank you for purchasing an Applewood book. Applewood reprints America's lively classics—books from the past that are still of interest to modern readers. For a free copy of our current catalog, please write to Applewood Books, P.O. Box 27, Carlisle, MA 01741, or visit us at www.awb.com.

The original spellings and punctuation used in the original quoted material have been preserved in this book.

978-1-4290-9640-9

PUBLISHER'S NOTE

In November 1870, Picturesque America was launched by American publisher Appleton & Co. as a "series of papers...consisting of splendidly-executed views of the most unfamiliar and novel features of American scenery." Over the next four years, nine hundred images and hundreds of thousands of words were sent out, by subscription, to a large audience. It was one of the first printed publications to celebrate an American nationalism based in the physical world rather than in the political or historical realm. Utilizing all of the modern methods of printing and distribution of the day, Picturesque America beautifully instructed Americans how to think about their country. Physically and emotionally torn by the Civil War, America of the 1870s needed healing. Picturesque America gave to Americans a way to envision the seemingly unchanging landscape of the country at a time that celebrated advancement, science, and discovery.

We are today a bit wary of progress and the ways that we use our precious land. We are concerned about climate. We see landscape as something humans have the power to destroy or to protect. We look backward and see simpler days. The handmade books that we are publishing as part of our Picturesque America series are made from the images and words of hope sent out over a century and a half ago. Our America is different—today, we celebrate and preserve what is beautiful and needing of our protection.

—Applewood Books

BOSTON.

THERE was little of the "picturesque," to the eyes of the Puritan colony which took up its abode on the main coast where now stand Charlestown and Bunker Hill, in the bold, bald, bleak, triple-hilled peninsula which confronted them on the southwest. It is true that one effusive Puritan, with peripatetic habits, wandering in the late spring-time in the neighborhood, found it possessed of "fair endowments," the hillocks "dainty," the plains "delicate

Brewer Fountain, Boston Common.

and fair," and the streams "clear and running," and "jetting most jocundly." His less imaginative brethren esteemed the promontory bare and drear, even in the season of budding and flowering Nature; for one of them describes it to be "a hideous wilderness, possessed by barbarous Indians, very cold, sickly, rocky, barren, unfit for culture, and likely to keep the people miserable."

The Puritans named it, with prosaic sense, "Tri-Mountain;" the Indians called it, with poetic suggestiveness, "Shawmut," or "Sweet Waters;" and the gratitude of its earliest settlers, who came from old Boston of the fens of English Lincolnshire, christened their new abode "Boston." The Charlestown colony, like the children of Israel, suffered from exceeding want of water, and moved to Tri-Mountain, which they purchased of its reverend owner, Blackstone, for the absurd sum of thirty pounds, because of the "sweet waters" which the Indian Shawmut promised. Thus began to exist Boston, with its teeming memories, its dramatic history, its steady growth, and its manifold picturesque and romantic aspects.

To him, however, who approaches Boston by the bay, it is difficult to distinguish the three hills upon which Winthrop and his fellow-colonists perched themselves. The city wears the appearance of a single broad cone, with a wide base lining the water's edge for miles on either side, ascending by a gradual plane to the yellow-bulb apex afforded by the State-House dome. Only now and then is the plane broken by a building looming above the rest, and pierced by the white, pointed steeples or fanciful modern towers of the churches, or an occasional high, murky, smoke-puffing, brick chimney rising amid the jumble of dwellings and warehouses. Boston presents the singular contradiction of symmetry in general outline, and irregularity in detail. One scarcely imagines, as he gazes upon this almost mathematically cone-shaped city, rising, by equal and slow gradations, to its central summit, that it is, of all places, the most jagged and uneven; that its streets and squares are ever at cross-purposes; that its general plan is no plan at all, but seemingly the result of an engineering comedy of errors; that many of its thoroughfares run so crazily that a man travels by them almost around to the point whence he started, and many others run into blank no-thoroughfare; and that, by no process of reasoning from experience otherwhere, can he who sets out for a given destination reach it.

The visitor who reaches Boston, indeed, by water, can hardly fail to be struck with the natural beauties—heightened now by artificial adornment—of the harbor, narrowing, as it does, in even curves on either side, dotted with many turfy and undulating or craggy islands—long stretches of beach being visible almost to the horizon, now and then interspersed by a jutting, cliff-bound promontory, or pushing out seaward a straggling, shapeless peninsula of green. Almost imperceptibly, the coast of the noble bay vanishes into villages—now upon a low, now a lofty, shore—which, in their turn, merge as indistinctly into the thickly-settled, busy suburbs, and the city itself. The islands, which in Winthrop's day were bare and wellnigh verdureless, are now mostly crowned with handsome forts, light-houses, hospitals, almshouses, and "farm-schools"—edifices for the most part striking, and filling an appropriate place in the varied landscape. Fort Warren and Fort Independence—in the former of which the Confederate Vice-President Stephens, and Generals Ewell and Kershaw, were incarcerated—are imposing with their lofty ramparts, their yawning casemates, their sharp, symmetrical outline of granite, and their regular, deep-green embankments. Nearer rise, from a lofty hill in South Boston, the great white sides and cupola of the Perkins Institution for the Blind, which Dickens so graphically described after his first visit to America To the right of the State-House dome looms, distinct and solitary, the plain granite shaft of Bunker-Hill Monument. Below, on either hand, are the wharfs and docks, crowded with craft of every size, shape, and nationality, from the little fishing-yachts which are wafting, on a summer's morning, in large numbers hither and thither on the water, to the stately Cunarder, whose red funnel rises amid the masts in its East-Boston slip. An eye-glance from the harbor takes in nearly the whole of the Boston shipping. It is modest, compared with the forests of masts and funnels which cluster along the East and North Rivers; but its extent and movement give evidence of a busy and prosperous port. The water-view of Boston betrays its industrial as well as its commercial character. Large, many-windowed factories, tall, smoke-stained chimneys, appear at intervals throughout the stretch of thick settlement from City Point, in South Boston, in the south, to the limits of East Boston and Chelsea, in the north, indicating the weaving of many fabrics, the fruits of deft handiwork, and the transformation of the metals to useful purposes.

Scene in the Public Garden.

On its harbor-side, Boston exhibits its trade and industry, its absorption in the businesses of life, the sights and scenes of engrossing occupation. Transferring the point of view from the eastern to the western side of the city, the results, instead of the processes, of wealth appear. From the arch in the steeple of the Arlington Street Church, you gaze upon one of the most striking and noble scenes which any American city presents—a scene of brightness, beauty, luxury, adorned by the elegances of horticultural, architectural, and sculptural art, enriched by the best effects of native taste, and gifted by Nature with fine contrasts of elevation, declivity, and outline—a scene which includes all that of which Boston is most proud in external aspect. In the immediate foreground lies the Public Garden, on a space redeemed, within a quarter of a century, from the waters of the Back Bay; for, up to that period, the waves reached up nearly to the edge of Charles Street, which separates the garden from the Common. Without possessing the pretensions of Central Park or Fairmount, the Public Garden is a gem of a park. It is not certain that now, in its days of young growth, it is not more lovely than it will be when its trees have grown into leafy arches, and its clumps of shrubs into opaque copses. Its edges are even now lined with thriving trees along the iron railings; winding paths lead in among exquisite flower-beds, umbrageous shrub-arbors provided with rustic seats, fountains playing in marble basins, statues of Washington and Everett, and commemorative of the discovery of anæsthetics, and "Venus rising from the Sea," about whose form the light spray shimmers. The borders of the lawns are adorned by beautiful combinations of vari-colored and vari-leafed plants. In the centre is a pretty serpentine, crossed by a heavy granite bridge, and upon whose waters there float swans and ducks, as well as canopied barges and queer little craft, let to the public at moderate prices. Close to the lake is a pretty conservatory, blooming with hot-house plants—the whole park being enclosed in a setting of spacious streets and mansions, park and mansions lending to each other the aspect of enhanced elegance. Beyond, almost hidden in its wealth of mature foliage, is the Common—the old, historic, much-praised, and laughed-at Common—rising, by a graceful plane, to the State-House at its summit, here and there interspersed with hillocks, whose sides peep through openings in the trees, and at whose feet are broad, bare spaces for military manœuvres and popular out-door games.

Behind the Common you catch glimpses of the steeples and public halls of Tremont [Tri-Mountain] Street; the historic steeple of the Old South, saved by a miracle from the great fire, which stopped under its very shadow; the steeple of the Park-Street Church, only less memorable in the annals of Boston; the comparatively plain, old Masonic Temple, now used as a United States court-house; and that noble and lavish specimen of Gothic architecture, the pinnacled, granite, new Masonic Temple, rich in decoration, and rising far above the surrounding edifices. On the left, the aristocratic Beacon Street—on the site of the cow-pastures of the last century—rises majestically toward the State-House—its buildings piled irregularly one above another, of brick and brown-stone and marble, of many shapes and colors—the street of the family and moneyed "high society" of the Hub. The view in this direction is most striking. To him who has gazed, at Edinburgh, from Prince's Street along the high, piled-up buildings rising to and capped by the hoary old castle, this scene of Beacon Street, with the State-

Old Elm, Boston Common.

House at the top, vividly resembles, in general outline and effect, that most picturesque of British cities. The principal difference is that, in place of the hoary keep and ramparts, there is the big, yellow dome, with its gilded cupola, and its American flag floating from the top.

Boston Common! Sacred to the memory of Puritan training-days, and the ruminating of Puritan cows; to the execution of witches, and stern reprimands of women branded with Scarlet Letters; to fierce tussles with Indians, and old-time duels; to the intense exhortations of George Whitefield, and the solemn festivals of the Puritan colonists; to struggles with British troops, and the hanging in effigy of red-coat foes; not less to the memory of thousands of lovers, dead and gone, from the time when it was the favored retreat "where the Gallants, a little before sunset, walk with their Marmalet-Madams, till the bell, at nine o'clock, rings them home!" A "small but pleasant common!" says old Josselyn, who saw it with his critical English eye, fresh from Hyde Park, just about two centuries ago. A small, perhaps, and certainly pleasant common, still, it is in these later days. Indeed, for more than two centuries the Common has been the lung of the town and city, the most central and the most agreeable of its open-air resorts, at once the promenade for grown people, and the play-ground and coasting-tryst of the children. Occupying a space of nearly fifty acres, there has been room enough for all; and, while the Common was long the outer western edge of the city, it is fast becoming its centre, as the spacious streets and squares of stately brown-stone and swell-front mansions are gradually stretching out upon the constantly-increasing "made land" of the Back Bay. The beauty of the natural position of the Common, and the richness of its soil, have required but little art to make it a charming park, gifted with all the variety and pleasant prospect worthy of a great and thriving city. It sweeps down the slope of the hill on the edge of which is Beacon Street, and at the summit of which is the State-House—broken, now and then, by undulations crowned by trees and carpeted with softest turf—until it reaches a lowest limit at Boylston Street, on the south. Its foliage no efforts of artistic cultivation can anywhere surpass. Many of the trees are centuries old. The noble rows of elms which, on the Great Mall running just below and parallel with Beacon Street, rise to a stately height, and, bending toward each other on either side, form a grand, natural, arched cathedral-nave, were planted one hundred and fifty years ago; while those of the Little Mall, running at right angles to the first, were set out by Colonel Paddock, rather more than a century ago. These are the two main avenues. The thick, cool shade is gratefully resorted to in summer; seats are ranged along for public use; here *Punch* revels in his quarrelsome squeak; and candy-venders, and lung-testers, and blind organ-grinders, and patent-medicine men, ply their out-door trades; and here the "gallants" still walk, as of yore, with their "madams" in the slowly-deepening twilight and the soft, moonlit nights. The Common is intersected by a maze of irregular, shaded avenues, its foliage being spread thickly over the larger portion of its surface; while its expanses of lawn, kept with assiduous pains, are as velvety and bright green as those of the boasted London parks. On every hand, the Common betrays evidences and memorials of its venerable age and its teeming history, as well as of the tender care with which it is maintained by modem Boston. In one corner is an ancient graveyard, with hoary tombstones, on which the inscriptions are half effaced, and which here and there lean over, as if at last weary of celebrating, to indifferent eyes, the virtues of the forgotten dead; and with embedded vaults, whose padlocks are rusted, and whose roofs are overgrown with grass and moss. Just behind the graveyard is a small, encaged deer-park, where the nimble and graceful denizens of the forest graze, or sleep, or eat, mild and tame, and apparently indifferent to the gaze of the curious passers-by, who linger a moment at the grating to watch their movements. Near the centre of the Common is the "Frog-Pond," a much-abused but pretty bit of water, provided with a fountain and a granite lining, situated just at the foot of one of the umbrageous hillocks, and always a pet resort for the children, who, in summer, sail their miniature yachts and frigates on its clear waters, and, in winter, skate on its glossy surface. Hard by the Frog-Pond is the still proud "Great Elm," a wonder of Nature, and a landmark of history. For more than two centuries its immense trunk and wide-spreading limbs have been the admiration and the shelter of Bostonians. An iron railing preserves it from rude abuse; an inscription tells of its venerable but unknown age, its historic significance, and perils by wind and storm. It is jagged and sear, but still stands vigorous and hale, with its circumference of nearly twenty-two feet, and its more than seventy feet of height; while the spread of its branches extends across eighty-six feet. Near by the Park-Street Mall stands the noble fountain given to the Common by Gardner Brewer, and appropriately called, after him, the "Brewer Fountain." It is an exquisite product of Parisian art, with a lower large and upper small basin, the water jetting from a topmost knob and through spouts in both basins, half veiling the bronze figures of old Neptune and Amphitrite, of Acis and Galatea, which sit in picturesque posture beneath. The fountain stands amid a cluster of noble elms; and above it rises the narrow and pointed spire of the Park-Street Church. At the lower or west side of the Common is a broad, bare space, where reviews are held, and base-ball games are played, the hillocks above converting it into a half amphitheatre, and affording a fine stand-point whence to view the displays and sports.

Leaving the Common, and passing along Beacon Street and by the Public Common, you reach the quarter of elegance and luxury and lavish taste which has sprung up entirely within twenty years, and is known as the "Back Bay." Penetrating this quarter, you have quite lost sight of all that is old, staid, and historic, about the Puritan capital. The aspect bespeaks forgetfulness of the past; it symbolizes Boston in its present and future prosperity; it tells the story of what fruit, in domestic luxury and architectural display, persistent thrift in commerce, and the busy competition in the active walks of life, bring forth in these latter days. The Back Bay is stately, without being cheerless; it is new, and not glaring; it is modern and ornamental, yet the substantial New-England character is impressed upon its firm, solid, yet graceful blocks, and broad, airy streets and squares. It stretches from Beacon Street, on the one side, southward nearly two miles, almost to the limits of what once was Roxbury; and here a vast area of residences—all of the better sort, and ranging from pretty, tempting rows of brick "swell-fronts" of two stories and French roof, for the family of moderate means, to great, square, and richly-adorned palaces of brown-stone—has been built in wide streets, and wider, tree-lined avenues, with now and then a statue, and oftener a church of the modern, showy Gothic or Flemish style. Mansard is the tutelar architectural saint of the whole quarter.

A sudden contrast is it to turn off from the view of this really splendid and brilliant quarter into cosey, umbrageous Charles Street, famous as the residence of Holmes, Andrew, and Fields, to pass up through the sedate repose and dignified presence of the "Beacon-Hill" district. Here, in Mount-Vernon Street, and Chestnut Street, and Louisburg Square, is the older aristocratic quarter, cast into a majestic shade by its plethora of ancient elms, notable for its tall "swell-fronts," with neat, small gardens in front, and carriage-ways up to the sombre doors. Many of the staid old families—the "high respectabilities"—continue here, disdaining the temptations of the brighter and more showy sphere of the Back Bay.

Out of this sleepily-tranquil neighborhood, on the eastern slope of the hill, you suddenly come upon the bustle and clatter, the wide-awake world of trade and shopping. The tide of business is caught at Tremont Street, to rise into a rushing, half-pent-up torrent on ancient Newbury, now Washington Street. And now you are in the midst of business, official, and historic Boston. In Boston, above all American cities, the charm of natural situation, and the painstaking of generously-patronized art, are enhanced by historic associations which will surely find a place in the great American epic of the future. In that part of it which lies between Tremont Street and the water are most of the memorable spots and edifices around which clings the aroma of past heroic deeds and noteworthy scenes. Here, too, are the buildings used for public purposes and the assemblages of the citizens—passing down School Street, the high, granite City-Hall, with its half-dome of the Louvre type, its singular complexity of architectural design, its broad esplanade adorned by the bronze statue of Franklin, and its appearance of busy absorption in municipal affairs; near by it is the historic, Saxon-towered King's Chapel, with the graveyard ensconced in the midst of the living bustle; and opposite the lower end of the street stands the yet more historic Old South Church, staid and plain, which Burgoyne turned into a riding-school for the British soldiery, after using the pulpit and pews to light fires, where

Jamaica Plains.

Whitefield preached and Franklin worshipped, and, since the great fire of 1872, serving the purpose of the post-office; and just around the corner from the Old South is the site of the house wherein Franklin was born.

The historic relics of old Boston—some of which, to be sure, have passed out of existence, swept away by the exigencies of modern convenience—are to be found scattered over the northern and eastern end of the peninsula; but the tortuous region included between the head of State Street and the northern limit is perhaps the most thickly studded with memorable spots and ancient mementos. At the head itself of State Street, in the middle of the thoroughfare, stands the old State-House, a grave old pile, with a belfry, looking down gravely upon the haunts of the money-changers and "solid men," for whom State Street is the centre and nucleus, and now given up to tailors' shops, telegraph and insurance offices, lawyers' chambers, and the Merchants' Reading-room. Passing from State Street through a narrow lane, you come upon the most notable of Boston edifices, standing in a somewhat narrow square, surrounded by a constant and hurried bustle of trade, but preserving still the architectural, and, in a measure, the useful features of a century and more ago. Faneuil Hall, built and presented to Boston by Peter Faneuil as "a town-hall and market-place," is a town-hall and market-place still. It is a large, rather square, thoroughly old-fashioned building, with three stories of arched windows, surmounted by a cupola, which is all too diminutive in comparison with the rest of the structure. On the ground-floor is the market, which overflows on either side upon the pavements; the second floor is devoted to the great public meeting-hall, with galleries on three sides, a large platform opposite the entrance-doors, and, over the platform, the large and imposing picture, by Healy, representing the United States Senate in session, and Webster, on his feet, making the memorable reply to

Hayne. The walls are studded here and there with portraits of busts of eminent men, old Governors, and other Massachusetts worthies, among which may be recognized Faneuil himself, the three Adamses, Hancock, Gore, Sumner, Lincoln, and Andrew. Here are held all sorts of political and other meetings, orations, campaign-rallies, and general conferences of the citizens. The reader need scarcely be informed that it was in Faneuil Hall that the citizens of Boston were aroused to resistance against the British, and that many of the most memorable scenes in the earlier stage of the Revolution took place there.

Proceeding from this historic quarter southward by Tremont Street, and along the Common, one reaches, first, the ornate and imposing Masonic Temple, with its arched windows and lofty pinnacles; and, just beyond, is the stately, sombre-colored, substantial Public Library. At this point all the principal public buildings are left behind, and a newer Boston is approached. Those who are not yet beyond the climacteric of age can remember when the space which separated thickly-settled Boston from the suburb of Roxbury was but a narrow neck of land, which in some places almost converted Boston into an island, and whereon were but a few scattered wooden houses. Now, however, this part of the peninsula is as fully occupied as its more ancient quarter, but in a very different style of streets and buildings. The narrow neck of land has been widened by the filling in of new land, and now constitutes a wide, well-built reach between Boston and Roxbury. The whole quarter is called the "South End." The main thoroughfare, Washington Street, is, unlike its aspect in the west, wide, straight, spacious, umbrageous, adorned with many handsome buildings, marble hotels, the great new Catholic cathedral, and long lines of bright and tempting stores. The squares and streets are regularly built, and, but for the long blocks of houses constructed exactly alike, which give a monotonous appearance, the "South End" might well bear comparison for its beauty with the handsomest quarters of other cities. The "South End" has, however, plenty of light, air, and elbow-room.

The suburbs of Boston have been well compared to those of Paris; and Brookline, especially, has been called the Montreuil of America. The amphitheatre of the hills, in which the peninsula is set as in a frame, is almost circular; these eminences are undulating, rising now into cones, now into broad rotundity, broken here and there by jagged cliffs and abrupt descents, dipping deep into leafy valleys, and then sloping off almost imperceptibly to wide, flat, fertile plains. Nature has endowed this surrounding series of hills with all that could beautify and make picturesque; it is not a single circle, but many circles, of uneven elevations, one without the other; and, from many of the farther summits, the city, with the yellow dome and glittering cupola of the State-House at its apex, may be seen throughout its extent, enclosed in a magnificent framework of the foliage of the hills which intervene. Especially striking is the view of the city, thus enclosed, from Mount Warren, where the General, Warren, is buried. Mount Hope, Mount Dearborn, and Mount Bowdoin, the latter of which eminences stands just south of the old town of Roxbury. Upon the groundwork thus provided by Nature, all that in modern art and taste, and in generous expenditure, could conduce to elegance and luxury of aspect, and comfort of residence, has been added to the landscape. Almost all the Boston suburbs are fairly bedded in rich foliage, much of it comprising the old forest-trees, and much also due to the careful cultivation of succeeding generations. Perhaps nowhere in America are the English arts of lawn and hedge culture, of garden decoration, more nearly imitated, or more successfully. There is the greatest variety in exterior adornment, as there is in architectural design. In the midst of large areas of lawn and copse, the square, compact, little-ornamented, sloping-roofed mansions of a century ago are followed by imposing, newly-constructed mansions, with fanciful French roofs and towers, an amplitude of verandas, and the protuberance on all sides of jutting bay-windows. In some of the suburbs are estates which would far from shame an English duke who dated from the Conquest; with their roods of hedge lining the roads, their broad avenues, winding through ravishing prospects for half a mile before reaching the mansion, their large conservatories and cottages, their close-cut terraces, and their gardens abloom, in the season, with rare flowers and a wealth of native shrubbery. Any of the suburbs may be reached by rail from the centre of the city within half an hour, and most of them in half that time; and here the heads of old families and the "merchant-princes" delight to vie with each other in the beauty and refinement of their home-surroundings. The suburbs of Dorchester, which overlooks the harbor, and of Roxbury, next west from Dorchester, both of which are now included within the city boundary, occupy the higher elevations in the immediate vicinity of Boston, and, although so near, afford many retreats where one may easily imagine himself in the depths of the country. Both are built on the sides and summits of rather jagged and irregular hills; and, if we once more compare Boston with Edinburgh, and the State-House to Auld Reekie Castle, it may be said that Roxbury well represents Calton Hill. It is the most thickly settled of the southern suburbs, and has a pretty and busy business square; advancing beyond this, you walk along shady streets, taking sudden turns up-hill, or plunging downward with an easy or sharp descent.

Next beyond the eminences of Roxbury, the almost, flat expanse of Jamaica Plains is reached. But the beauty of the plain, lying coseyly and shadily among a circle of hills, with pretty streams flowing through it, with a grateful variety of home-like residences, wide, airy, and tree-lined streets, and a snug appearance which is even more perceptible here than upon the heights, is not less attractive than the more lofty suburbs. Many a quiet, rural nook, where the idler may sprawl upon the yielding turf, and angle, meditate, or read, forgetful of the nearness of the big, bustling metropolis, or even of the more contiguous suburban settlement, may be found just aside from the village of Jamaica Plains.

The most attractive spot in this suburb is a placid lake, lying between the plain on one side and sloping hills on the other, fringed with overhanging foliage, broken here and there by well-trimmed lawns, which stretch down from picturesque cottages or old-fashioned mansions to the water's edge, with now and then a bit of sandy beach. Here take place, in summer, suburban regattas and much boat-rowing, while, in winter, "Jamaica Pond" is a pet resort for Boston skaters. Just beyond the Pond, the loveliest of Boston suburbs, Brookline, is reached. Brookline, on its southern side, comprises a series of beautiful highlands, occupied almost exclusively by large, handsome mansions, in the midst of spacious and picturesquely wooded parks. It is a snug, highly-cultivated, home-like environ, the favored retreat of the Winthrops, the Lawrences, the Sargeants, and other of the older and wealthier Boston families. Its streets are broad, and wind in and out under elms, maples, and chestnuts, presenting changing aspects of elegance and luxury at every turn, charming bits of landscape suddenly appearing between the trees, and lordly residences of brown-stone, brick, granite, and wood, disclosing themselves at the end of arched avenues, and on the summit of graceful eminences. Sometimes broad lawns sweep down the hill-sides to dead walls facing the streets; sometimes only the cupolas and turrets of the mansions peep above the thick copses. It is hard to conceive any style of picturesque architecture in which Brookline is wanting, from the Elizabethan to the Mansard. Nor is it without historic edifices: one house, the ancestral

College Buildings.

residence of the Aspinwalls, which still stands in a wide, open field, near the centre of the town, sturdily supports its two centuries' existence. Brookline is as noteworthy for the beauty of its churches as for the air of luxurious comfort which its residences betray. The avenues leading from Boston "Back Bay" through Brookline are the favorite drives of the city people, and, on pleasant afternoons, are crowded with showy turnouts, horseback-riders, and family carriages. The old reservoir occupies the crest of a noble hill, and the drive around it is full of pleasant prospects; while the new reservoir, "Chestnut Hill," lying on the northern edge of the town, is surrounded by broad roads along the granite embankments, and affords an agreeable limit to the drives from the city. The public buildings of Brookline, mainly consisting of the new Town-Hall and the Public Library, are striking for the tastefulness of their design, and their combination of beauty and convenience. Both are in the French style, the Town-Hall being lofty, of granite, and capped with a high Mansard façade. The Public Library is a snug little edifice of red brick, with Mansard roof, and having a pretty, close-cut lawn in front. The village square, lined with tall brick and wooden stores, is one of the brightest and pleasantest of the many village squares around Boston. At one end of it is the railway-station, whence trains start every hour for Boston, reaching it in fifteen minutes, and returning quite as frequently; and from the square, in all directions, the streets branch off irregularly, invariably lined with shade-trees, and betraying the evidences of domestic taste and comfort.

Beyond Brookline the river Charles flows through flat, marshy tracts, westward from the Back Bay, to the hilly districts of Waltham and Auburndale, some miles beyond; and, on its northern bank, lies the University of Cambridge, situated on a broad plain, extending from the Charles to the eminences of Somerville. Cambridge wears the same aspect of umbrageous adornment, spacious streets, and elegant mansions, characteristic of all the Boston suburbs; and, nearly in its centre, is Harvard University, with its various edifices standing, without apparent order, in a spacious and shady park. Here are plain, old, brick dormitories, built more than a century ago; bright new dormitories, with much ornament; a Gothic, granite library, Gore Hall, with pinnacles, buttresses, and painted windows; the picturesque Appleton Chapel; the cosey Dane Hall, where the law-lectures are given, with its heavy pillars and severely plain front; the square, marble recitation-hall; the solid granite anatomical museum; and other large edifices of various styles, for the different uses of the university. The high elms, forming majestic natural archways, the quiet that reigns throughout the scholastic purlieu, the singular contrasts between the new buildings and the old, the rare collections which have been gradually formed for generations, the venerable age of the university, its illustrious catalogue of alumni, its noteworthy share in the history of the nation—all render a visit to "Old Harvard" one of peculiar interest. Beyond the colleges a broad, winding thoroughfare, Brattle Street, leads past comfortable and sometimes very handsome dwellings, in somewhat more than a mile, to the beautiful, hilly cemetery of Mount Auburn; but, on the way, several places of note are to be observed. One is the grand old mansion now occupied by the poet Longfellow, memorable as having been the headquarters of Washington during the siege of Boston, a large, square, wooden mansion, painted yellow, with a veranda under wide-spreading elms at one side, a garden behind, and a pretty lawn extending

Mount Auburn Tower.

to the street in front. The next house beyond was occupied by Dr. Worcester, the compiler of the dictionary, till his death; while, farther on, toward Mount Auburn, down a cool, shady lane, is the house, not very unlike Longfellow's, which is the ancestral home of the poet Lowell. Branching off from Brattle Street, Fresh Pond, a lovely expanse of water, much resembling Jamaica Pond, is reached; and thence it is but a brief jaunt to the most beautiful of New-England "cities of the dead," Mount Auburn. This cemetery is built on the sides and summits of graceful hills, and in the shaded valleys between them; and, while Nature has been lavish with foliage and picturesque prospects, art has bestowed every various and appropriate adornment. There are lakes and ponds, elaborate tombs and monuments, nooks and grottos, and an abundance of flowers, quiet paths beside modest graves, and, on the summit of the highest hill, a large gray tower rising above the trees, whence a panorama of Boston and its suburbs, for miles around, opens upon the view. Beyond Cambridge is the new suburban city of Somerville, built on the side of a hill, and then comes the long, flat city of Charlestown, with the granite shaft of Bunker Hill looming conspicuous and solitary among its mass of buildings, steeples, and chimneys. This, with Chelsea, completes the circuit of the Boston suburbs; and, after one has made it, he cannot but confess that the Pilgrim wilderness has been made to blossom like the rose, and that no American city has been more amply blessed in the beauty, comfort, taste, and picturesqueness of its surroundings.